T0147125

Wake Up to
YOURSELF

Wake Up to Who You Really Are—A Powerful Creator

PAUL KNOX

BALBOA.
PRESS

A DIVISION OF HAY HOUSE

Balboa Press books may be ordered through booksellers or by contacting:

Balboa Press
A Division of Hay House
1663 Liberty Drive
Bloomington, IN 47403
www.balboapress.com.au
1 (877) 407-4847

Because of the dynamic nature of the Internet, any web addresses or
links contained in this book may have changed since publication and
may no longer be valid. The views expressed in this work are solely those
of the author and do not necessarily reflect the views of the publisher,
and the publisher hereby disclaims any responsibility for them.

The author of this book does not dispense medical advice or prescribe the use
of any technique as a form of treatment for physical, emotional, or medical
problems without the advice of a physician, either directly or indirectly. The
intent of the author is only to offer information of a general nature to help
you in your quest for emotional and spiritual well-being. In the event you use
any of the information in this book for yourself, which is your constitutional
right, the author and the publisher assume no responsibility for your actions.

Any people depicted in stock imagery provided by Thinkstock are
models, and such images are being used for illustrative purposes only.
Certain stock imagery © Thinkstock.

Print information available on the last page.

ISBN: 978-1-5043-0078-0 (sc)
ISBN: 978-1-5043-0079-7 (e)

Balboa Press rev. date: 01/04/2016

CONTENTS

INTRODUCTION

Now, I have to say that this way of thinking and the Ideas, (I was going to say new Ideas but they've been around since the dawn of Man) I've read in all the books that I've accumulated over the years on this way of thinking were very foreign to me. I grew up a typical Aussie Bloke. I am a Traddie, I played Rugby League growing up, I went out with my mates and got drunk, sometimes got into fights (which I never started by the way) and done some things I would rather not mention!

I was engaged twice and have two fantastic boys from each relationship; Blaine and Dylan and am now Married to a beautiful person, Marina, and have a great Stepson, Noah, and a beautiful fur child called Teddy, our dog.

I have lost nearly everything I own twice after each separation from the engagements and had to both times move back in with my Mother in my early and late twenties. (by the way, I don't blame anyone for these things happening...not anymore)

When I was nineteen my cousin who came to live with us when I was about five (he was around ten) committed suicide, he was like a brother more than a cousin, we use to do everything together. Two years later I lost my

Grandmother who I was very, very close to because my parents were divorced when I was around six years old due to my Father being an Alcoholic. My Mother worked two and sometimes three jobs at a time to support us so I spent a lot of time with my Beautiful Grandmother. I went through depression a lot of the time and would have been ecstatic at certain times in my life if I just didn't wake up, I remember thinking... *there's worse things than dying!*

In saying all this, I don't believe I was deprived of anything growing up, or have had a hard life. I had a very close and supportive family and fantastic friends. I only mention these things because I know when I started this journey and started reading books from different teachers, I used to think... *yeah, but your successful because your you, it was probably just your fate to be successful,* even though most of these teachers had a lot more hardships in their life then I did. Then I would think that's why they have a great life now, because they had such a hard childhood or have had more struggles in their life than the average person. It's funny the excuses you come up with when your life isn't the way you want it to be.

So I just want people to realize that I am just like most other people with a similar story to 90% of the world's population. I'm not famous or well known in any way, although I am regarded as a reasonably good plasterer around Ipswich!

the only difference is, I started asking questions and opened my mind for the answers, and, like I've heard and read so many times...*when the student is ready, the teachers will appear.*

In The back of the book there are a few blank pages for notes, I would recommend that you take note of the teachers I mention throughout the book and have a look at their books and the other tools they have to help you on your journey, like they've done for me on my own journey. I would also recommend that you try out the things I've learnt and shared in the book, put them into practice and see if they help you in anyway, what do you have to lose?

So...without any further ado...this is my journey of waking up to myself - of waking up to who I really am.

I hope you can get something out of it

1

In The Beginning

<u>30th June 2009</u>

Up until about twelve months ago, I wouldn't have described myself as one of these self-help type of people or on any sort of journey. I was going through a bit of a bad time, sick of my job, not enough money coming in to pay the bills sometimes, let alone have any sort of fun life. Basically the same story millions of people around the world have, just a struggle to get out of bed in the mornings, and it still is, this isn't one of those stories about "the struggle" and the wonderful life I have now, I haven't got there…yet, but I'm sure I will. This is a work in progress.

I have a job which I am really starting to hate, I am a plasterer and the last couple of years have been really bad, work-wise, just seems to be less and less work around and the economic crises doesn't help. We have our house on the market because of the amount of pressure we're under financially.

Spiritually, I have always only had a really firm belief in three things, a belief in God, (I'm not too sure what God is but I don't think of this grey- haired, long-grey bearded old man sitting in his thrown judging people), that everyone has a spirit and that we go to a better place when we die. I've thought about thousands of other things, like why we're here, do we have a fixed destiny? can we change things? All the questions most people have, but the only three things' I'm sure about in my own heart is that there is a God, we all have a spirit and we all go to a better place when we die... if we have treated people the way we would like to be treated, in other words, try and do the right thing as much as we can.

I can't personally except what some religions believe about committing sins, I think we're here to experience all things, why would a God create us and the Universe, send us here and then punish us for experiencing the things that are on the very place it created? and why would it create sinful creatures? and why create something it thinks is so beautiful and of the image of itself to destroy it? or even worse...send his/ her creation to an eternity of suffering in Fire and Brimstone because you committed some sin which was interpreted (by man) from the Bible to be a sin. And which interpretation of the Bible (by man) is the right one. It just doesn't sit right with me because I am a Father and even if my sons killed another person, I would be unimaginably upset for the victim's family and absolutely disgusted, embarrassed and greatly disappointed in them, but if I am honest with myself, I could never destroy them or stop loving them let alone send them to an eternity of suffering, even if they didn't ask for my forgiveness. I would like to think that I would never talk to them again, disown them, maybe even pull the trigger on them myself but I know deep down, I couldn't do that. So, when I think about some religious beliefs, they just don't sit right with me.

But, in saying that, good on people for having their beliefs if it helps them get through their days on this planet, more power to them.

About twelve months ago my wife Marina came home with this DVD that her friend Lisa lent her and she said to me, *"I want you to watch this DVD"*, I said... *"what is it"*, *"It's sort of about positive thinking and this law of the Universe called the Law of Attraction"*, I said to her.... *"It's some self-help crap"!* my exact words were... *"I'm not watching that shit "*, she said, *"just watch it for 10 minutes if you don't like it we'll turn it off"*. *"Fair enough I said"*.

After watching it for 10 minutes, (at first, I didn't really trust the way I was feeling and didn't want to let on to Marina how I was feeling either), but I thought to myself- *Wow, this all makes sense to me, there could be something in it.* Needless to say I watched the whole thing... and watched it again... and again for six or seven days in a row. It really hit me somewhere deep inside and I couldn't understand why, but I do believe that if you watch or read something or someone is explaining something to you, if you personally feel there's some truth that hits you in the story, there might be some message in it for you.

The DVD was called *The Secret*, but that wasn't the be all and end all of what I wanted to know. *The Secret* just introduced me to this Idea of the Law of Attraction and eventually it led me to other books, DVDs and teachers, and on the journey I'm on at the moment, which I have to say is a very interesting and exciting one. Even though I'm not happy with my job or my financial situation, I'm far from the happiest I can be at the moment, but every new book I read or DVD I watch, I know I'm getting closer to that great place I want to be and it's not just me on this journey, my wife is as well which is great, because when I have really bad days or weeks or months, my wife talks about the things we've watched or read and gets me back on track, I try to do the same for her but I have to say that she has a lot more positive times than me, but I'm getting there....slowly.

We've also watched some great DVDs and read some fantastic books on living the life you want. Two teachers I've discovered are Abraham (Esther and Jerry Hicks) and Louise Hay.

They've taught us a lot of helpful things that we're starting to practice. We've been trying hard to visualize the life we want, believe it can happen and put into practice all the things we've watched and read, and little things have happened. One thing is that we don't worry as much as we use to about paying the bills anymore, we just know that when we need the money, it will come from somewhere and it usually does, things like that happening are just little ways that the Universe is saying.... *see it is true, I am here to help you and make your life what you want it to be, all you have to do is trust in me...don't worry, trust instead that I will give you what you want.*

So now, even though my life isn't what I want it to be, and I still have a lot of the...*why me!* Days, I just try to remember how the money to pay a bill just comes from somewhere if we don't have it, like a parent offering to lend money until we get money I'm owed from jobs, or someone wanting a job done just before a big bill is due. There's lots of ways money can come to you... you just have to trust that it will, and I'm starting to, I just want to get to the place where I'm doing something I love and don't have to worry about watching my money, to be financially free so my wife and I can really start to enjoy life. I'm willing to try and think differently, read inspiring books and watch DVDs to get the tools to make my life better if that's the end result. At the moment I think things aren't going in the direction I want them to because I am really not happy with what I am doing, I have read that you have to be happy where you are before you can move on, but I just can't when it comes to my job so I'm stuck at the moment.

I am trying to trust that the universe will give me an opportunity to do something I love and am passionate about.

2

The Relapse

Well, it's been about a year since I've written in here, a few things happened that made me go back to my old, negative ways of thinking so not a lot has changed in my life.

I went off the whole Law of Attraction thing for a few months, but I've started watching more of the Abraham DVDs from Esther and Jerry Hicks and DVDs from Louise Hay, I think I'm back on track again.

One thing that helped me was that Abraham says that things we don't like happening to us happen because it makes us more clear about how we want our lives to be, a bit like we wouldn't know warmth if we didn't experience cold, or wouldn't know happiness if we didn't experience sadness, that sort of thing, and when it gives us the clearer and better version of the life that we want, we have to try and focus on that and not the cause of the clearer perspective or where we are now, the present situation is only temporary.

Our next door-neighbor Kim is a Reiki Master and she holds seminars in a little Temple that her Husband, Jess, built in the back yard. We've also done a couple of seminars and that has helped us a lot. It taught us a lot about our energy and how it can be used, it also made us feel a lot calmer. We really do feel a difference in ourselves after doing the Reiki Seminars.

Marina and I are so hungry to learn all we can about different aspects of the Spiritual side of things, I believe it can only help us on our Spiritual Journey.

I've also made peace with my job although I don't want to keep doing it for the rest of my life, I'm just trying to trust that the Universe will bring me something else, until then I'm happy doing what I'm doing. I was worried about just accepting my job and letting go of the angst and worry of doing it for the rest of my life because I thought it would send the wrong message to the Universe, but by excepting where I am at the moment doesn't mean I can't bring into my life what I want, it just frees me up to focus on my dream life and I also believe that whatever our experiences are at any moment in time is what we're meant to experience to help us when we are on our life purpose. So life experience is a tool to call on and use later, when we need it.

I've also decided to stop worrying about where the next job is coming from and just trust that they will keep coming, and they have. We still have our house and we're keeping on top of the bills, It's still not perfect but at least we can pay our bills.

3

The Tides Are a Change'n

It's been steady-as-she-goes for the last five months or so, work has been fantastic, I've been having trouble keeping up with it, which is great. We're on top of our bills and have actually been able to buy a few things for ourselves which we haven't done for a few years.

I think the biggest thing I've learnt in the past five months is to keep trying to just trust that things will work out, trust that the universe will bring me what I need, that's the only thing I can put all this work coming my way down to because the financial crisis isn't over yet and I have talked to a lot of tradesman who are giving it away and looking for different jobs. The only thing I have done different is to hand my worries to the Universe, or God, or whatever you want to call it, and say... *you take care of it, I'm sick of worrying!* And If I'm being honest, I have to say that the Universe is taking care of it. It's like when you're a kid and your worried about something, and being a kid it seems huge, you tell your parent or your guardian your problem and they say.... *I will take care of it, don't you worry about a thing, I will sort it out*, and you feel like the planet just fell of your shoulders. It's the same feeling when you say to the Universe... I have had a gutful; you take care of it. Someone once said- *The shortest prayer in the world is... F#@k it!*

I know some people would think... *this fella has lost it, he should have been living his heyday in the flower power years, he would've fit right in!* I have to tell you that I would have thought that to, but I'm putting some of these theories to the test and it seems to be working, probably not as fast as it would work for some people, for me it's a bit of a choppy ride, but only because of me.

I let those negative little leeches get a hold of me sometimes, until I feel them sucking the life out of me and it prompts me to start thinking positive again, basically because there's nothing else I can do.

When you've had enough of your life, you try everything you can to turn it around or just give up, you only have two options and that's them, and just giving up (I don't mean suicide!) or letting go seems to work.

4

The Little Things

I don't have any exciting news like I've made it, I'm living my dream life...Damn it!

Work has gone a bit quite the last 2 weeks but I have a couple of good sized jobs before Christmas so that'll help.

We always get a bit excited around this time of year, besides Christmas coming up, we go camping at North Stradbroke Island in early January for a couple of weeks. About four families go and we have an absolute ball, last year was probably the best trip yet. When we first got there last year the Ranger said to *us "good luck finding a spot"* (we thought... *yeah, thanks for that Mate!*) because the place was packed. You can't book one particular spot you have to find a 6meter x 6meter spot where ever you can find one. In one part of the park you can camp right on the beach front, we thought it would be gone for sure because it's the best spot in the park, but when we got there people were packing up to go, we couldn't believe it, we all got side by side in the best spot you can get and the place was packed, sometimes the universe is kind!! We didn't have any expectations and we got the best spot. Although, before we went, I was looking at the map of the park and thinking how great it would be if we all got a spot beside each other right on the beach, and then forgot about it.

I've read that you have to live from the end, in other words, if you would like something in your life, feel like you already have it, imagine what it will feel like to have the thing you want and imagine it like it already exists, which, (unbeknownst to me at the time) is what I done. I looked at the camping map and imagined that those camping spots were already ours, it was a done deal. I've also learnt that you can't strangle that image, in other words, don't keep thinking about it until you start worrying that it won't happen, always imagine it as a done deal that can't be undone, feel the excitement of it, feel the butterflies in your belly and then let it go, so the Universe can go about his/her work and bring you your dreams.

It only seems like a small thing, but I think the Universe always works the same way, weather you think it's a small thing or a big thing, it's all the same to the Universe, it's only us that makes it a big thing or a small thing.

5

A New Interest

The trip to Straddie wasn't as good this year, we had torrential downpours most days but we did have a few good days, it was the worst floods in Queensland since 1974.

Not much has changed in the last 8 months or so. We do have a new interest. Marina and I have just been sick of going to work…coming home…paying the bills…. going to work…coming home… paying the bills…etc.… etc.…etc.

We both decided we need to have an interest that we both enjoy and start to try and enjoy life a bit. I asked her if she has ever had an interest in something or if there is anything she would like to do in our spare time.

She said she's always been interested in photography, she actually done work experience at high school with a photographer. I've had an interest in photography ever since I was young as well and we both love going for walks in the rainforest and in nature so we bought a camera and we've been doing that for about 4 months We absolutely love it and we go to different National Parks as often as possible. We got a couple of photos blown up and printed and took them to a framer, he said if he frames them for us he could hang them in the Gallery that he rents next to his shop to see if we could sell them, we said *"that would be great, thanks"*; not expecting too much to come of it. After a month or so we got a call from him saying he sold 2 of our prints; how excited do you think we were! We couldn't believe that someone liked our photos enough to buy them.

After that we thought that maybe we should do something with it, so we have started going to weekend markets, we have a great time at the markets, just the whole atmosphere of them are fantastic. We haven't made a fortune but have sold a few prints and nearly everyone that sees our prints all say how beautiful they are which is worth going just for the positive feedback.

We have really found a passion, something that we truly love to do, we could be in the rainforest all day taking photos and not get bored, time just seems to stand still while we're in the rainforest taking photos, that people like them is just a bonus.

6

Ask and It Is Given

We've been going to the markets for over a year now and still really enjoy it. We've sold a few more of our framed prints and still get just as excited as we did when we sold the first one. We've added other things to our stall which helps us with the cash flow. It gets a bit tiring because we still have our full time jobs and do the markets every Sunday and every second Saturday. We have met some really nice people at the markets who do it as their full time job. They've told us about some annual festivals that are held at different times of the year in different towns which we go to, we meet up with them all in the different towns and go out for dinner and talk about the day we had and just to catch up. It's been so good for us, just breaking the monotony of going to work…coming home…going to work…. coming home!!!

We really needed to find something we love to do to break the mundane life we we're stuck in and we did, we ask the Universe for an interest, something we love to do and we got it, it would just be nice if one day we could make a good living from something that we love to do.... C'mon UNIVERSE!!

We always have such a good time because we go away for the weekend, get to explore different towns, catch up with friends and it's all payed for by the money we make at the festivals, it's been fantastic!

Besides that, escape every now and then, not much else has changed, we still struggle to pay the bills sometimes and we still don't like our "day" jobs all that much, but we're continuing to work towards a better life.

I have to say, our lives have improved over the last few years, slowly but surely and I do believe it's because we've changed the way we think, I really can't put it down to anything else because the only thing we've changed is the way we think.

In saying that, we have a long way to go before we're living our perfect life but our lives have definitely improved.

7

A Punch in The Face

I haven't written in here for a long time because nothing much has changed, we don't do weekend markets anymore because it just got too much with going to our full time jobs as well but we still do annual Festivals, on average only 1 every few months. We still love going for walks in the rainforest and taking photos, it's our saving grace, it's the only thing I've found I can do that Instantly makes me feel better, as soon as I walk in the rainforest all my stress seems to melt away.

Our financial situation as gotten better, we're still working towards doing something for a living that we're passionate about but that just hasn't happened yet.

We just came back from a holiday where it was just Marina and I, we haven't done that since our Honeymoon. We usually have our holidays with other people which is great but it was just nice going away with just the two of us.

We went to this beautiful little place on the Sunshine Coast called Montville, we've been going there for a few years now just for a weekend or day trips, any chance we get really, we call it our happy place, it's a bit like when we go into the rainforest, as soon as we get there all our stress seems to disappear, we would love to live there one day.

Something happened on our first day there which is a good example of why I think it's taking so long for us to have the life we want.

Last year was the best year (financially) that we've had in probably 5 years, we were so excited to be in this beautiful place that we love for the next 10 days, looking forward to going to all the National Parks around the area and excited about all the great photos we'll get and all the other things we were going to do. And then my mobile phone rang, it was our accountant ringing saying that we will probably have (give or take a few hundred dollars) a twenty-thousand-dollar tax bill…. now I had to tell Marina this!!

I got off the phone and told her straight away so I could get it over with, she actually took it really well. *"It's ok"* she said…" *we knew we would probably get a big tax bill this year…what can they do? we'll pay it off"*. all this time I could just feel my blood reaching boiling temperatures and then it happened… the explosion. The F's and the C's were flying…." *That's it F###ing Universe…you can get F####ed best year we've had for years…. I start to really believe in you and start feeling happy…what do you do…. you come over, punch me in the face and say get back down there…yooooou prick"*!!!!

this went on for a little while but I eventually calmed down; with help from Marina and also being in Montville helped a lot, I would hate to think if I got that news at home!

Anyway, that's why it's taking so long because things like this seem to happen, everything is going great (not perfect because I'm still doing the same job) for a while, something happens and bang, here come the old negative thoughts and back to my old ways of thinking for a few months. I know it's me and I even know what I'm doing wrong, and how I should just think…. well, it's ok, I put my trust and faith in the Universe, it will guide me through it. I'm also a believer in the Idea that everything happens for a reason, we experience the positive and the negative for a reason, maybe to use that experience in the future, but It's hard when things like that happen, I know I still have a lot to learn.

The next day we went into the Village to a great little shop that we always visit when we're there called *Cadman Cottage* which sells a lot of, what I like to call, self-growth material as well as other great stuff, and Marina found my savior which was a book by an Author and teacher by the name of Dr. Wayne Dyer. The book is *Wishes Fulfilled*.

All the material I've read on this subject so far by Louise Hay, Abraham and also books by Mike Dooley have all been great books and DVD's and have all helped me in their own way and have been invaluable, but when I read this book by Dr. Dyer it just all started to come together. For instants, I've heard of the belief that we're all one, we all come from the one Universal source, which I sort of got but didn't really grasp, I couldn't really get my head around where the power to manifest our lives comes from and if I couldn't understand that then it would probably be hard for me to manifest things into my physical world. I've also had this long held belief that I'm having such a crappy life now because of bad Karma, I must have been a really bad person in a past life and now I'm paying for it, I think that has probably been the biggest setback in my life; that I don't deserve a good life because of my bad karma, or maybe I was born at the wrong time maybe I should've been born at a different time and place. Funny how utter nonsense becomes so real, so concreted into your belief system, even though I have absolutely no Idea who I was in a past life! I wasn't even really sure if we had past lives but I still thought that's the reason for my life as it was.

But when I read how Dr. Dyer explained it, I got it. He explained that we are all intended (or thought) into the physical by the same source that created the universe and everything in it the same way, by thought and intention. So, if God or Source or whatever you want to call it created us from itself, there is no mistakes, God doesn't make mistakes, and we must be a part of the same energy and have the same power to create with our thoughts and intentions as God does. And because of that we create everything that happens in our life, even the negative things, so we can't blame anyone or any circumstance for anything that happens to us. I have read that before to but I just wouldn't except that I attract _everything_ to me, even the so called bad things.

Man O Man…that is so powerful for me! That's how I understand it anyway.

I always had this Idea that we were all separate from God but thanks to Dr. Dyer, I understand now that we are all connected not only to God but to every person, creature and *every- thing* not just in our world but the Universe because that is what everything came from and this energy that runs through us must run through everything because it is where all things come from.

I also understand now that the energy that we are or the God part of us is by far the more important and more powerful part of us, not our physical flesh and bones. If I can just learn to ask the universe for what I would like to manifest in my life from that God part of me, where all my power is, I know I have the power for it to come into the physical world, because the same Source created the whole Universe and everything in it, including me.

It's funny because other teachers have explained this but for some reason the way Dr. Dyer has explained it and everything else he has explained in his book, I understand, I really get.

Just by understanding this I have started to think about a lot of other things as well. I truly get now that our thoughts are powerful and they create our lives because that's how God created the Universe and everything in it, by thought and intent, including me and I am part of God so I must have that same power. It makes me feel so powerful, and in awe of God and what he gave me, and of all the things it created, but not in an arrogant way because everyone has this power so I don't feel like I'm better than anyone or anything else, how can you be better than anyone if they are made of the same and by the same energy…or what I like to call God.

8

My Beliefs

I've been thinking about my beliefs lately and I'm pretty lucky that I didn't grow up in a devoutly religious family because it has given me the freedom to explore different beliefs without prejudice. I did go to a Catholic primary school and was baptized so I was taught the Catholic beliefs at school, but I remember thinking how I didn't understand a lot of it, it just didn't make sense to me. But on this Spiritual journey I'm now on, a lot of those things I heard back in primary school and things from the Bible through the years, make sense to me now, they didn't then because I was thinking purely from a physical point of view, and I believe a lot of religions interpreted their religious books from a physical point of view.

For example-

God is in all places at once. I use to think, *how?* if we are made in the image and the likeness of God, then that means he is like a physical person. I pictured God as this grey haired, long grey bearded old man, sitting in his thrown in heaven, judging people, deciding who's been good enough for him to grant them their wishes. To me, even that is a physical interpretation...judging people, I can't imagine God doing that or punishing people and sending them to eternal hellfire. I don't believe in a vengeful, angry God, all those behaviors are physical behaviors and I believe that's why the religious powers that be interpreted God that way, because they are thinking from a physical point of view, not a Spiritual point of view which God is.

Its fear based and God isn't fear, Source energy is love...that's all, nothing else...pure love, love can't be vengeful, angry, judgmental or any other negative thing, love is love.... That's it.

So I thought, how can God be in all places at once if he's sitting in his thrown in heaven, it's imposable.

It is imposable...physically imposable, but I've learnt what God is; God is energy, Source energy that everything in the Universe is made of and comes from, an intelligent energy that can be in all places at once and is all knowing, the primal intelligent energy that permeates through the entire Universe and everything in it, just like the air around us that is everywhere at all times. Source energy, or God, created everything, from itself, there is nothing it didn't create which is where we get our power from to create our lives the way we want it, we are created from this Source energy, we are God in physical form. Even scientist say that you can look at any physical matter, including us, and if you have a powerful microscope

22

you can see that everything is energy vibrating, matter is vibrational energy slowed right down. That's how I interpret the line- made in the image and likeness of God.

It also explains when Jesus said- *Have I not said that you are all Gods.* He said that because we are, we are made from Source energy, we are a piece of God. I used to think that was blaspheming, Man O Man, you can't say that!!

Jesus said…*Have I not said you are all Gods!!*

Jesus also said- (not an exact quotation, but who knows exactly what he said). - *All the things I have done you can do, and more.* How can we? …. Because we are made from Source energy, God in physical form which gives us the power to create whatever we want to experience.

Another one is- *All things are possible with God,* Why? …. Because we are Source energy and when we know that for sure, when we realize and believe in who we really are, all things are possible because we are a piece of God.

I've also thought about how God said to Adam and Eve not to eat from the tree of knowledge. I use to think *why? Isn't knowledge a good thing.*

I've come to learn that too much knowledge can suppress the spiritual side of you, which is the most important part of who you are. I believe when God said that, he meant, don't believe everything you see, hear and are taught, believe in your own gut feelings which is your spirit communicating with you, letting you know if what your taking in is truth or not, if it resonates with you, great, if not, let it go, follow your heart.

The proof is in the pudding, God warned us, *don't eat from the tree of knowledge*, most of the world's population has done exactly that and still do, and look at the state of parts of the world now and what we do to each other!

This is why I also don't believe we were all born sinners because Adam and Eve ate from the tree of knowledge, the tree of knowledge is a metaphor for all of us to not take in too much worldly knowledge, it can kill the spirit. God was saying take in Spiritual knowledge to remind yourself of who you really are…Source energy in physical form, powerful creators ourselves with free will to create whatever we want to experience in our lives.

You have dominion over all things, why do we? …. Because we are Source energy, but also because we are conscious beings with free will and the power that God gave us to choose and create our lives the way we want it, I don't believe it's up to God to decide whether or not it is going to let us have the life we want to have based on how often or how well we have worshiped him/her and if we're worthy enough, God gave us the power, free will and dominion over all things so we can create our own lives the way we want it to be, we have dominion over all things because God wants for us what we want for us and I believe he gave us dominion over all things so we can create heaven on Earth, for ourselves and the people around us.

I truly don't believe we are born sinners, we are not separate from God, we are made by and of God, how can we be sinners? We are Source in physical form.

In a part of the Bile it tells a story (this isn't the exact words) of a man going to the disciples and asking them to cure his son who suffered from severe epilepsy, because Jesus told his disciples that they have the power to cure illness and cast out demands but the Disciples couldn't cure the man's son so he went to Jesus and asked him to cure his son, which he did, when the man left the Disciples asked Jesus why they couldn't cure this man's son and Jesus said-*"Because of your unbelief, for assuredly I say to you, if you have faith, you will say to this mountain, move from here to there and it will move and nothing will be imposable for you"*

I believe that that message was for all of us not just the disciples, as I believe all Jesus' messages were for all of us, he was leading by example, he was showing all of us that we all have the power to create whatever we want as long as we believe in who we really are and in our power to do so.

What you believe is so important in finding your Devine purpose and creating your life the way you want it, like the saying goes- What you believe you will achieve.

9

Let Go and Let God

Another thing I think that has been holding me back is not letting go of how things will manifest. In Mike Dooley's books he calls it the *"cursed how's"*. His books are great on teaching you how to let go of the how's of your wish list. It just comes natural to most of us that if you want something, the next step is to work out how to get it, but now that I'm starting to understand how the Universe works, and how powerful our thoughts are (by the way, scientist can actually measure a thought, so a thought isn't just a thing we think, it is measurable action) I'm getting better at letting go of the how's and letting God take care of the how's, as Mike Dooley says, *"the how's are the domain of the Universe"*. But he also says that doesn't mean we can just sit in our lounge chairs at home and expect what we want to just fall in our laps, we have to move in the general direction of our dreams, like - researching what we're interested in, look at courses or buy books about it, things like that, and get out in the world so the Universe can engage us. I think what he means by That is, you can't bump into the right people or see things that inspire you, or experience coincidences and serendipity's (which are all just the Universe engaging you) things like that, if you're just sitting at home visualizing, you have to move in the general direction of your dreams, do what you can, with what you have from where you are at that moment and the Universe will take care of the rest. It can't open doors for you if you're not there to walk through them, just like automatic doors won't open if you're not there to trigger the sensors.

In the movie *The Secret*, Bob Proctor said that if you do just a little research on successful people, you'll learn that even though they knew what they wanted to achieve, they didn't have any Idea how they were going to do it, they just knew they would achieve it.

I read a saying in Dr. Dyer's book which has helped me so much...*Let go and let God*, how good is that! Like I mentioned earlier, it feels like the planet has dropped off my shoulders when I say that.

I've always believed that there's two parts to us, our flesh and bone part (ego) and our spiritual part (our God self) but now I realize just how much more important and powerful our God self is, It's the real part, it's us, it's who we are, it's our connection to our power. After our bodies are gone, it lives on so it's the real you. I've learned that we only need a thought of what we want and a feeling of having it now without any doubts that the Universe is powerful enough to bring it to us, that's how God created everything, and we are a part of God, so we must have that power as well. If we can just push aside our ego that says our flesh and bone part needs to work out how to bring into our lives what we want so the Universe can work out the how's for us. Our God self knows how to get whatever it is we would like to come into our lives because it is connected to everything in the universe, we just have to move in the general direction when we can and *"let go and let God"* (that's my new favorite affirmation) if we want to live the life of our dreams.

My ego self has ruled my life, thoughts like; I have to get a good paying job if I want a happy life, even if I don't like doing the job, or if I don't have a house and nice things I'm a failure, or, what will people think if I do this or that. What I've noticed and learned from reading these books is that all the truly happy and successful people think from their God selves, in other words, they follow their heart and intuition and do things in life that their passionate about, and they don't care if everyone else thinks their crazy, the money and all the nice things just follow, and they let God take care of the how's. Our God self will give us the life we want if we let it. I've noticed that the more I've been trying to follow my heart, the more connected I feel to the Universe, I'd love to just quit my plastering business and trust in the Universe but I have bills to pay so I'll just think and feel like I already live my dream life and it will come. Dr. Dyer calls it living from the end. As I mentioned earlier, for things to manifest in your life you have to think and feel like you already have them now, like Mike Dooley says... *"Always and only dwell on the end result"*

I've learned that the Universe gives you exactly what you ask for and think and feel about, so if you have a thought of wanting something, it will give you wanting it for has long as you 'want' because the feeling of want is not in the now.

For me that is fantastic because when I think about my past, God has given me exactly what I have thought and felt about, including the bad stuff, so I'm starting to learn to think and feel abundant, prosperous, healthy, and that I have a career that I am passionate about, now, in the present, even though it's not here yet because wanting is always in the future and never comes.

I think the hardest part will be having the staying power to keep thinking this way, but my motivation is that if I don't, nothing will change, I read somewhere that the definition of insanity is- ***Continuing the same behavior and expecting a different result.***

I'm determined to start living from my God self.

10

Staying Connected

On the way to work this morning, I was trying to think of ways that I can really believe and feel that my God self is in charge of my life, and while I was driving my Ute I thought to myself…my flesh and bone body isn't driving this Ute, my spirit, or my God self is driving, it's in charge now, and at work I kept thinking that my God self is doing everything…walking, talking….knowing what to do next and what's coming next and whatever does happen every second is exactly what is meant to happen because my God self is in charge of my life now. It's funny because I'm still doing the same job which has made me feel so trapped and freedom-less but since I've been thinking this way I feel such a sense of freedom, don't get me wrong, I still would like a career that I'm completely passionate about and can't wait to get out of bed in the morning and get stuck into, but now I have more of a sense that my current job has been good to me and given me the things

I have now and when I first started (especially when I started working for myself) I had a sense of purpose and gratitude for being able to have my own business. But now It's time to move on to my real purpose in life, It's time to move on, to do what I'm really here to do and I know that the Universe will guide me to it if I just keep thinking and feeling that my God-self is in charge of my life now not my ego-self and try and look for and follow the guidance it gives me, things like coincidences and serendipity's, the Universes guidance tools.

I have felt a definite shift in me, It's like I just have this knowing that everything is going to work out even better than I can imagine because my God-self is in charge of my life now Thinking like that has really connected me to my Source and when I consciously think that everything I do and everything I say or imagine is my God-self doing all this now not my flesh and bone self, I feel freer then I ever have.

Just to bring me back to my awareness that God is in charge, if I'm in town or whatever I'm doing I say to myself, "where are we going now God, over there? no worries mate, let's go, you're in charge! Another little trick I've learned to try and feel that connection to the Universal source is; if I'm sitting outside, I try and imagine my spirit expanding out and touching a tree in the distance or even a cloud in the sky or if I'm inside, I imagine my Spirit expanding out and touching something in the distance, like the TV or a picture or a figurine, it seems to work for me.

If anyone ever reads this, they'll think I'm a lunatic, but it works!

11

On Reflection

<u>20th February 2014</u>

I've been looking back at my life a bit lately, just to see what my thoughts have manifested in my life, and I was thinking about my plastering career.

After I separated from my fiancée about 18 years ago, I was working in a sheet metal factory, even though I met some great friends there (who I'm still in touch with today) the money wasn't great and I just wasn't happy with the Idea of working in a factory for the rest of my life, not that there's anything wrong with that, I just knew it wasn't for me. After the separation, I lost my job, which was completely my own fault, I was taking sickies because I was depressed and I just dreaded the thought of having to go to that factory for the next 8 hours, let alone the rest of my life. Luckily my Mother has a 2 story house with a flat downstairs and she has always supported me when I needed it, so she let me stay there until I got on my feet again.

I started to think about what I could do, I thought about my Father, (who I didn't know very well, my parents separated when I was 6 and I didn't see him much) who was a solid plasterer and a lot of his family were solid plasterers so, I thought maybe I could be a plasterer, not a solid plasterer just a plasterer, I knew it wasn't a passion of mine but then again I didn't think that way back then, I just wanted a good job and I thought I could get a trade and maybe have my own business one day.

When I think about my thoughts and feelings about it back then, I had no doubt that I would Achieve it. I done a six-month prevocational course at my local college and started doing little jobs for family and friends, then I became good friends with the manager of the store where I bought all my materials, he started getting me little jobs and I started helping other plasterers with their jobs. I started to learn more and more from the other plasterers and got more and more confidant with my work and within 2 years I done my trade test and passed, I was a qualified plasterer and got my BSA license. Not long after I got my license, I started my own business.

Now, I didn't do a traditional apprenticeship, I didn't have a car...I borrowed my Mothers Hatchback Laser to do these little jobs and I even had to make my own hawk (the square thing you put the plaster on) because I didn't have the money to buy one, but when I met my friend Mark (the store manager where I got my materials) he helped me get a trade account with the company so I could get the things I needed. I just done little jobs for friends and family and other plasterers taught me things when I worked with them and I have everything I have now thanks to plastering, and the people that the Universe brought into my life so I could achieve my Goal.

Now that I have read all these books about creating your life the way you want it, it really is true, when I think about that one thing in my life, (having a trade) the Universe brought into my life all the people and circumstances I needed to achieve my goal and that's just one thing in my life, all be it a pretty big life change for me.

Even though like I said earlier, I am grateful for my trade and my business, and to all the people that God brought into my life to make it what it is today, I am ready to move onto making a living doing something that I love and am truly passionate about. I just don't know what that is yet, but I am going to let go and let God bring it to me.

I felt a bit guilty about feeling that way…achieving my goal of being a tradesman and being a business owner and now wanting to move on, but I read that it is natural to want to achieve more in your life. Who you really are, which is a spirit…a part of God, is expansive…it is part of the whole Universe so naturally it wants to expand, it wants to experience everything it can so that's why, when you achieve one goal, you set another one, the Ego part of you tells you it's wrong to think that way…you should just be happy where you are, that's the equivalent to caging in and restricting your spirit, that's what causes depression, anger, sadness and all these other negative feelings, the God part of you is saying….keep experiencing and expanding.

The best part of life I think, is achieving a goal you set for yourself and not just a small goal you set because you're too afraid to set a big goal, I mean goals like a new career, financial abundance, perfect health or any other thing you really desire. If there's one thing I've learnt from these teachers, it's to not live in fear of failure of anything, like it says in the Bible... with God, all things are possible and I really believe that now, especially after I look at the things I've achieved without knowing any of this. If you want to achieve something, act like it is already manifested for you, act like your living it now and really believe in your soul that that is who you are now, try to think that way as much as possible and eventually the Universe will take care of the rest. I have to remind myself that sometimes things won't change straight away, I have to realize that I've been thinking a certain way about certain things for a long time and when I change the way I think about some things, it takes a bit of time to change, there's lag time, just like a ship needs time to turn after the wheel is spun, but eventually you reach a point of critical mass, a point of no return and you're on your way, the flood gates open.

From what I've learnt, the only thing that stands in the way of your goals is inpatients and doubting the power you have to realize them. How can you doubt your power when you are a piece of God and connected to the whole entire Universe which has all the answers to every request that exists...if that's not power, I don't know what is and it is in you to use and create whatever your heart desires... Ask and it shell be given!

Evan though I am not living my dream life yet, looking back at what I have achieved so far, I know this is the truth, it is real, it's not just wishful thinking, it's real.

Now I know who I really am... a part of God, not apart from God, with the power to create my life the way I want it, I feel more confident of reaching my goals in life, no matter what they are. I've reached a lot of goals I have set for myself, most of them I don't consider to be big things, and all of them without the knowledge I've learnt over the past six years, but I am starting to set bigger goals for myself now that I am starting to relies who I really am, I feel like my life is just getting started.

12

AIB'S

25 March 2014

I'm going off on a bit of a different tangent here, but since I've got this new realization of who I really am and more of an understanding of how vast and powerful God really is, I've been thinking a lot about another subject that I've always been fairly open minded about- Advanced Intelligent Beings on other planets.

I've been thinking how The Universal Energy, or, God fits into this picture.

To start with, scientist have said that there's more stars in the Universe then there are grains of sand on all the beaches of the world, and a certain percentage of them must have planets orbiting around them, so to me you would have to be pretty arrogant to think that we're the only Intelligent life in the Universe and why would God create this infinite universe with only one planet which has Intelligent life. I think God created Intelligent life thousands, tens of thousands and maybe even hundreds of thousands of years before us.

Some people say that there might be Advanced Intelligent Beings.... (I say Advanced Intelligent Beings because when I say "Aliens" I think of sinister little beings that want to come here, get rid of us all and take over the world...but that's just me!) or AIB'S (I'm getting sick of writing Advanced Intelligent Beings!), on other planets but how would they traverse the vast distances of space. Now I don't pretend to be the world's smartest bloke, but it makes sense to me that if their thousands of years more advanced than us, then I'm sure they have got the technology to travel around light-years of space very quickly, if not instantly. To them, it might be like going for a drive to the local shop.

So then I thought...why would they come here? Well, this is where I come back to God.

If there are people on our planet today that are only just starting to connect to the Universal energy, or, God (which created everything in the Universe, including life on other planets) for guidance in their lives and also guidance for their purpose in this life, If AIB'S are thousands of years, or even only hundreds of years more advanced than us, maybe they can communicate with the Universal energy like we talk to our parents or teachers for guidance, and maybe, just like God works through us for the benefit of all life on this planet and the planet itself, maybe God works through AIB'S as well.

As far as I know, there is a missing link in our evolution. Now, what if it was God's intention for the AIB'S to come to Earth and manipulate our DNA (which would explain the missing link) to give us self-awareness and conscious thinking so that we could use this power that is within us (that we have because we are a part of God who used this same power to create the Universe and everything in it) so that we could consciously create our lives, the way we want it, using our free will, and also so we could consciously make the world a better place. So basically what I'm saying is, we were born with the power inside of us to create our world the way we want it, but, God, through the AIB'S, gave us the ability to do it consciously.

I know that the majority of the world's population still don't realize that we are all connected to each other and to everything in the Universe, and don't realize the power that we all possess to make our world heaven on Earth, but we're starting to, and I'm sure the AIB'S have known this for a long time, and if by any chance this theory might be true, The AIB'S probably thought… *I hope the big fella knows what he's doing!* especially when you look at the way we treat each other sometimes.

Thinking this way sort of makes me feel obligated to do everything I can to create a happy life and in my own small way, try and make the world a better place, otherwise this power I have to create the life I desire and the gift of self-awareness and conscious thinking that God gave me (maybe through the AIB'S) has gone to waste, or, like a saying in Dr. Dyer's book- *"I don't want to die with my music still inside me"*, it seems to me that that might be as close to a sin as you could get.

It all sounds a bit crazy, but once upon a time, everyone thought the world was flat and that the Earth was the center of the Universe, so you never say never.

If this did turn out to be fact, to me, it wouldn't take anything away from the way I think of God, in fact it would make me be more in awe of God and Sources' greatness and power and also mighty grateful that God also created me, with this power to create my life the way I want it, not that I'm not already in awe and grateful.

13

A Bad Day

I know in the past I've been patchy and up and down with putting into practice the things I've learnt but the last three months or so, every day, I have made a conscious effort to think positive, feel the way I will feel when I have the life I want to manifest, and I am even at the stage where sometimes it really does feel like I'm living the life I dream of. But when after years (admittedly in patches) and especially after months of every single day putting into practice the things I have learnt, nothing happens (in regards to my job), I start to lose that positive feeling and It's hard to get myself out of it, especially when I feel like my job is just grinding me into the ground, each day deeper and deeper, no matter how I think or feel. When I say nothing happens, I mean to keep me going, little things, I don't expect to have my dream life over night, but it would be nice if little coincidences, or small serendipity's would happen or maybe new people coming into my life that might (maybe unbeknownst to them) give me an Idea of my purpose in life...just anything to keep me on this path but it's just not happening. I don't know what I'm doing wrong, maybe this doesn't work for everyone, maybe some people just have a fate that comprises of struggle and disappointments, after all, there's a lot of people like that in the world and people in a lot worse situations then I am, and I'm sure they think positive sometimes, maybe more then they think negatively, like me, but, like me, little things don't seem to happen for them to keep them thinking positive so they can realize their dreams.

Maybe this is all just wishful thinking after all, I don't know anymore but I'm just about ready to give up.

I just wish things would happen, things that I know are sent from the Universe, and are saying to me....'your situation is starting to change, just keep going'.

But.... nothing, not even a whisper.

14

The Markets

14th July 2014

I was pretty down there for a while but isn't that life? you just have to keep going, what else can you do.

I have found something that I enjoy doing, and if you asked anyone who knows me they would never in a million years think that this would interest me in the slightest. It's day trading! I actually discovered that I really enjoy doing this about five years ago but never thought much about it because for one, I knew nothing about day trading and it seemed so complicated and also, you need thousands of dollars to day trade.

Over the years I've had this fleeting curiosity in the back of my mind about the stock market but never really done anything about it because it just seemed like you had to have a lot of money to even think about it. I decided (just out of curiosity) to search on the Internet about trading the stock market and came across Information about a derivative of the Markets called CFD's (Contract for The Difference). You only need to have a percentage of the cost of the product you want to trade because you don't actually buy the product, you only buy (or sell) the price. I don't know the exact ins and outs of it, all I know is that it's exactly the same as trading products on the stock market but you only need a fraction of the money up front because you don't actually buy the product, and I know I enjoy it, I'm not sure why I enjoy it, but I do.

The biggest downside is that it's a highly leveraged product so even though you can make a lot of money, you can also lose a lot of money and pretty quickly, but to me that just means you have to be even more disciplined and careful with your trading plan. In saying all of that, according to the experts, you still need at least $5000.00 to start trading, which I don't have, not to lose before I know what I'm doing anyway, so what I've been doing over the past 5 years is I've been putting a few hundred dollars into my trading account when I've got it just to practice and to work out a trading plan and I think I'm starting to work out what my trading plan will look like. I know over the years a few hundred dollars here and there adds up, but it's cheaper than a University degree and I hate studying!!

I use to get really disheartened because I would have more loosing trades then winning ones but I've read a few books on day trading now and even the best traders have about a 50/50 success rate on their trades, but their successful because they get out of their loosing trades quick, before they lose too much money and they let the winning trades run, or add to them, that's why you need at least $5000.00 in your account so you can absorb the loosing trades until you have the winning ones, I won't go into it all here, but I've learnt a lot over the past 5 years.

I really think it is a passion for me, because if I wasn't passionate about it, I wouldn't still be trying to succeed at it 5 years later, and it's not the money you can make, I haven't made any yet, I just love trading for some unknown reason.

When I look back at what my perfect way to make a living would be, it is perfect, I can still work for myself, I can work from just about anywhere if I wanted to, as long as I have access to a computer, it would give me (and Marina) the financial freedom to start enjoying life, and most important of all, I really enjoy Day Trading...who would have thought!

Marina and I have discovered a few things that we enjoy doing over the past few years which is exactly what we asked for, maybe one day, something we enjoy doing will put us on the path to our dream life.

15

The Salon

A couple of years ago Marina started her own business, she's a hair dresser and she's done a few different things in the industry, she's managed shops, taught at a collage and the last thing she done was as a color technician which meant she had to drive for hours at a time to different salons teaching girls how to use this company's products. Evan though it was a great job for her, after a while I could see that all the driving and big days were starting to get to her and she said that it was starting to as well. She would leave sometimes at 6:30 in the morning and wouldn't get home until 7 or 8 at night, and a lot of her day consisted of driving in heavy traffic.

I said to her... *"why don't you start working for yourself"*? At first she was hesitant because she didn't have a single client and the thought of it scared her, but my work was going better and I knew she would do well. She's a great hairdresser and she has a good rapport with people.

It took a while but she decided to do it. I built a little room for her under my Mother's house where she started. After a few months a friend of hers (who is also a hairdresser) was interested in renting a shop and asked if Marina would like to share the shop with her, Marina agreed and she hasn't looked back. A couple of months ago she opened her own shop and she is that busy that she can't keep up with it. She rents chairs to other girls and she has so many people ring her that she actually asks them if they would mind if one of the other girls could do it, so she has not only built her own business from scratch but she has helped the other girls build their businesses as well.

I am so proud of her, she took the chance even though the thought scared her and she has built a great business from nothing. (Not that this is important because the most important thing is that you enjoy what you're doing) but she makes more money than I do, actually, a lot more money!

If it wasn't for her business, we definitely wouldn't be able to go away for weekends and buy a few things for ourselves.

The down side is she suffers badly from dermatitis from the chemicals. She said that this isn't her life purpose but she says that it's where she's meant to be at the moment. She looks at it like a stepping stone. Like me, she doesn't know what her life purpose is but she is so much better than me at controlling her impatience and frustration.

Sometimes I feel guilty when my work gets quiet and I have a day or 2 off and Marina has to go to work, the old attitudes of…I'm the Male in this relationship, I should not only be working but I should be making more money than her! I should be a better provider! Once again that's that old ugly ego trying to rise above the pack, trying to dominate my spiritual side, my God-self, but I'm getting better at getting rid of those thoughts and just being grateful that it's working out for Marina and I know that one day we'll both be doing what we love, living our dream life, living our life purpose.

Funnily enough, one of the ways I got over these thoughts of being a bad provider and the guilt of being at home when Marina was at work was to tell my mates how successful Marina's business is, and how she now makes more money than I do, it somehow felt like a secret I didn't want anyone to know, but when I told my mates it didn't bother me anymore... strange but absolutely true.

We are both on this journey and over the years she has also been putting into practice what she has learnt and changed the way she thinks about things and her life has changed and is still changing as a consequence.

16

The Trading Traddie

I finally got some exciting news. Not long after I wrote in here last I put another couple of hundred dollars in my trading account, and, once again, got up to about $700.00, opened a few other positions, and then…. went all the way back down to around $50.00 and as usual, I went to a bad place and thought…that's it. I give up, It's obviously not meant to be! I'm never trading again!! But then, on the 17th of October 2014 (I'm not sure why, but I remember that date) I decided to have a quick look at the market (even though I always say I'm giving it away) and noticed that the US30 - Cash Index was at the bottom of its trading range and was starting to come back up, after arguing with myself for a while about putting yet another $150.00 in my account I thought, I'll put it in and just leave it, no matter what happens, I'll either loose it again or I'll make a bit of money and I won't open any other positions, just that one.

After a few days my balance went from a couple of hundred dollars to nearly a thousand, this is OK I thought, but I wasn't getting excited yet because I know what's happened in the past! Another week or so went past and I was up to around $2000.00 at that point I thought about adding more of the Index to my position, and I thought no, because whenever I have done that in the past, it went down so I thought if it gets to $3000.00 and the price breaks through the last high for that day, I'll add more. By December I was over $3000.00 dollars and added more to my position, now I was getting excited! I remember thinking that I nearly have that $5000.00 in my account that the experts say you need to trade CFD'S. In January I got up to $5000.00...holy crap!! I think this is it, the turning point in my life!! I wanted to tell Marina (she still doesn't know) but I was worried that I could still lose it all, I made a deal with myself, I thought if I get over $10,000.00, I'll tell her and then it happened...I went back down to $3000.00, here comes that bad place again...I thought, that'd be right, I got this far now I'll lose it all, I started getting too scared to trade at all but if I want to make more money I have to trade! Then the words I read in Mike Dooley's book were ringing in my mind...when you have a dream, only think of, and keep in mind the end result. Phew!! Thanks Mike!

I also remember reading in a lot of other books that if you hang on to something to tightly and worry about it all the time, you will lose the thing you want, like Mike Dooley say's...I'm starting to turn trading into a cursed how.

So after another mind battle I thought, I'll try and wait for what looks like a good opportunity and open some more positions. A couple of days later I opened a few more positions and, eventually, I got up to around $7000.00 but after that I went back down to $4500.00. For a while my balance was going up and down between about $4000.00 and $7000.00 but then, at the end of March I was over $10,000.00!! I was so excited! I couldn't wait to tell Marina! I said to her... *"come and look at my Demo account, look at my account balance"* ...thinking it was just my practice account she shrugged her shoulders and with a sarcastic tone said... *"yeah...that's great... what do you feel like for dinner"*! (I do cook too! Well, more like Microwave!) When she went back in the kitchen, I got up and said... *"hay Darl, don't get mad at me"* ... *"what have you done"*! she said to me like a worried Mother, *"well, a few months ago I put a couple of hundred dollars in my trading account and that $10,000.00 is ours, that's my Live account"* !!! she hit me in the chest and said... *"it is not"*!! I said... *"After all our financial struggles over the last few years, I wouldn't lie to you about that".* she nearly had tears in her eyes, and she said... *"I'm so proud of you"*, well then I had tears in my eyes!!

Since then, I've been up to a high of $10,500.00 but am now back down to around $7400.00. (the market has been going sideways for a few weeks, so I know I shouldn't be trading while it's doing that) My next goal is $20,000.00 The thing I'm really struggling with now is patience, I have always been a very impatient person and because I love trading, sometimes I just open positions for the sake of it, just so I can trade and I think that's why I go down $2000.00 or $3000.00 before I make $4000.00 or $5000.00, it's no good for my mental health!! I have to try and control the extreme emotional Highs and lows and take control of my patience. I have to start doing what I done right at the start…wait for good opportunities, even if that means I don't trade at all for days or weeks if I have to.

Even though I've made this money, I'm still not confidant, I'm still learning.

I'm so glad I've read all the self-help books I have, those teachers are helping me now with my trading. When I get in a bad place after my account goes down and I lose confidence, I read one of their books or just remember what they've said. Like Wayne Dyer (Who, by the way, is coming to Brisbane in August, we're going to see him, can't wait!) who said that you are a piece of God, you have the power of the Universe at your disposal. So now when I go to that bad place I just try and think to myself… the Universe is my trading partner, how can I go wrong!!

Just the other day I was in a really bad place, I went down to $7300.00 and I haven't made any money for about 3 or 4 weeks now, and I was starting to think that maybe this isn't it, maybe this isn't my long awaited change of life for me, if it is, I should be making more money than I am, I should be a better Trader by now. It's not losing the money that I worry about, it's coming this far, from $200.00, and not being able to trade anymore, that scares me.

I was re-reading one of Mike Dooley's books… *Leveraging The Universe*, and while I was feeling like this, I started reading where I'd left off the day before… you will not guess what the first paragraph I read said, it read…. *"I have a friend who started a brand-new career as a… wait for it…Stock Broker"*!!!

In his mid-forty's (I was 41 when I started practicing day trading), and has been wildly successful"

If that's not a message from the Universe, I don't know what is!

I hope one day I can say I have been a wildly successful day Trader; Mike Dooley might put it in one of his books!!

17

An Amazing Weekend

What an amazing weekend Marina and I just had, we went and seen Wayne Dyer in Brisbane, he had a 2-day Seminar called "I Am Light" and one of the guest speakers was Anita Moorjani who wrote a book called- *Dying to Be Me*.

It's a book about her NDE experience. She was in the late stages of an aggressive cancer and her husband, Danny was told to contact her loved ones because she wouldn't make it through the night. She not only came back from the other side, but all signs of the cancer in her body were gone after 3 weeks! I'm pretty sure They said that no one has ever come back from that late stage of an aggressive cancer before. Her book is about what she learnt on the other side, or, as she likes to call it- the other Realm, just an amazing woman.

Wayne Dyer was just as amazing, the things he talked about were just so powerful. It's been great reading all these books, and they've helped me so much, but to actually see a teacher in person...you just can't explain it, you have to experience it, we will definitely be going to more.

It couldn't have come at a better time for me. Last Friday I went down to $3000.00 in my trading account and I was devastated...absolutely devastated, I took $2000.00 out just so I wouldn't lose it all, I have $1000.00 left in there to trade with. The old negative thoughts came back.... *Why God, why would you let me get so far... over $10000.00 and take it all away!!! Why...why...F##@ ing Why*!!!

Like I had nothing to do with it!

We done a guided meditation while we were there as well, it's called Isha Kriya, you can download it off the Internet so Marina and I downloaded it and we've been doing it every night. We have both felt a lot calmer during the day. I think Meditation, Reiki, anything like that can only be good for you if it calms and relaxes you and helps you connect to your source. I believe you have to be open minded to different things if you want to change things in your life for the better, being open minded doesn't mean you have to take everything you hear about on board, if it doesn't resonate with you, let it go and move on, but don't just discount things without trying or thinking about them first, you never know what gift you'll find by being open minded.

Amongst other great things Wayne Dyer was talking about at the seminar, he was saying that challenges in your life are there to inspire you to greater heights, the Universe will sometimes bring you down so you can get inspired enough to springboard you to a higher place. He also said you should do something because you love it and don't cling to outcomes, do it because you love it, not because of the results you think it is going to bring. That's exactly what I was doing, but then somewhere along the way the more I made, I started thinking, *what if I lost it all now, I couldn't handle it.... I would be devastated.... All my dreams and hopes for the future would be shattered...I would just give up.... This is my ticket to freedom!* then I started thinking, *I have to make money every week if I want to do this for a living, how can I do this full time if I can't even make a decent wage every week*, I was also really worried about letting Marina down, even though I know it wouldn't worry her. I put so much pressure on myself and it wasn't fun anymore, all I started thinking about, was failing.

I also done the one thing that Mike Dooley in his books says you should never do, I turned it into a cursed how. In my mind it was the one and only way I was going to get to where I want to be in my life and in doing so I tied the Universe's hands. There are an Infinite number of ways the Universe can guide me to my life purpose, to my Dharma, and by me focusing on this as being the only way, I restricted the Universe. I have to keep an open mind and not turn things I enjoy into a cursed how all the time, even though I can't see the way to my dream life, God can. I have to trust the process and trust the Universe.

I remember when I first watched *The Secret*, Jack Canfield, the Author of *Chicken Soup For The Soul* said, your life is like driving your car at night with the headlights on, you only have to see 200 feet in front of you....and the next 200 feet...and the next 200 feet and so on to get to your destination, you don't have to see the whole journey. To me, that means just taking baby steps in the right direction with what you have from where you are at the time. I'll just keep doing things I enjoy when I can and trust the Universe will get me to my Dharma.

I can honestly say that after this weekend, hearing Anita Moorjani's story and listening to Wayne Dyer speak...I honestly don't care if I lose the money in my account or get it all back and more. Man O Man, if I hadn't grown as much as I have Spiritually over the past few years I would have been suicidal if I made $10,000.00 and lost $7000.00, I hate to think of what the old me would have done, that's a blessing in itself!

I'm just going to do it because I enjoy it, not for any particular outcome and besides, I reached my Goal of $10000.00, (by the way, I have read that when you what to reach a goal, it helps to say at the end...*this or something better*, so you don't restrict the Universe) and we've still got $2000.00 in our holiday account that we didn't have, can't complain about that.

If Day Trading isn't what I'm meant to be doing at the moment, then something else is out there for me when the time is right.

Dr. Dyer read out this great saying by Patanjali
He said-

When you are inspired by some great purpose, some extraordinary project, all your thoughts break their bonds, your mind transcends limitations, your consciousness expands in every direction and you find yourself in a new, great and wonderful world, dormant forces, faculties and talents become alive and you discover yourself to be a greater person by far then you ever dreamed yourself to be.

So, I think I've learnt a great lesson, do something because you love it, not for what you can get out of it, and don't turn interests into a cursed how!!

Wayne Dyer also explained how, in the grand scheme of things, our planet, let alone our physical selves, are a tiny little speck in the Universe, (which we are all connected to) and if you truly believe that you are an eternal spiritual being... (which I have truly come to believe we all are) this life is the blink of an eye. When this life is done, and I know that I am eternal, and a powerful creator, and could have created anything I wanted, am I really going to worry about the little bumps in the road, or am I going to say to myself... *I wish I knew who I was and how powerful I was when I was in that physical body, I would have never worried about little things like that, I would have achieved anything I wanted to*...well, I'm still here!

Talk about thinking from the end!

18

The Great Man

Last time I wrote in here I was saying what a fantastic weekend we had at the Wayne Dyer Seminar in Brisbane. This morning on the way to town Marina read on Facebook that Wayne Dyer passed away in Maui Saturday night (Maui time).

We are in shock, only a few weeks ago we meant him and shook his hand, he was saying that he hasn't felt better in his life, he seemed so healthy and energetic. Even though we didn't really know him, we feel like we've lost a close friend, Marina actually cried that's the effect this amazing, amazing man had on people. He helped changed so many people's lives and touched millions around the World to say that he is going to missed by millions is an understatement.

This is one of my favorite sayings by the great Man-

When you change the way you look at things, the things you look at change

RIP Dr. Wayne W Dyer.

19

The Day Off

10th September 2015

I had the day off today and I've been feeling a bit flat lately so I thought I'd take Teddy (our fur child) to Colleges Crossing, it's a Nature reserve beside a river and they have picnic areas and a nature walk, just a really nice place.

When I was there watching teddy run through the water and just soaking up nature, I was thinking of the things Wayne Dyer was saying at his Seminar, (I don't want to offend anyone by saying this) but I really felt like he was there with me, and it made me think of how Anita Moorjani said when she was in the other Realm, she felt like her energy could be in a lot of different places at the same time, so I really believe he is with a lot of people, he touched so many.

I was thinking about how he was saying that our spirit is eternal and that we are NOT Human Beings Sometimes Having a spiritual experience, but we are

Eternal, Spiritual beings sometimes having a physical experience. He was also saying that everyone has a Dharma, a divine purpose.

The last few days my job has been getting to me amongst other things, and sometimes I get impatient and frustrated because I just can't seem to find my purpose in life. I've tried to do things that make me happy and things I enjoy doing and waiting for opportunities to arrive that might get me out of what I'm doing and on to my life purpose and just letting things unfold the way their meant to but sometimes, when your caught up in life, and just not happy with the way things are, it's hard to do that, let alone think of all the things I've been trying to put into practice that I've learnt over the years, I just want to find my Dharma!

But then, sitting on that log next to the river watching Teddy, I thought of Wayne Dyer's words...***we are eternal***, and I thought... *really, the only things that matter in this life is the experiences I gain, not the problems or the worries, they'll all go with this life and who I really am will move on with all the experiences I've had in this life and exist for eternity, and probably experience another physical life again sometime with even more experiences so bumps in the road in this life really aren't worth getting upset over.* I'm starting to realize how important thinking and living from your spiritual self and not your physical self is, and I don't mean airy fairy stuff in the sky, or locking yourself away in a monastery somewhere for ten years, I mean putting things in perspective, Spiritual perspective, because that's the real perspective. I stress less and I don't worry about things as much when I take the time to do this, because, like I said before, this life is the blink of an eye, all our problems will vanish with it and I believe the experiences will remain.

So then, I thought, well, what's the point of life? I think the point is to follow and realize your dreams, to experience the ecstasy of achieving a goal and living a happy, blissful life all the time, not just sometimes, living heaven on earth, finding your Dharma. I'm starting to realize that that is what life is about, following your heart and living your dreams, because I don't think I was born to experience struggle, stress, worry disappointment and unhappiness all the time and then die, what's the point of that? why be born at all?

It also makes it easier to understand that we do have the power to create our life the way we want, otherwise there would be no point to life, I don't believe we come here to suffer or experience disappointment and just let life happen to us without having the tools to change the situation that make us uncomfortable, like I said, what would be the point of that? I think problems we come across in our lives are the Universe's tool to keep us on track, to say to us...*Hay, you're getting off track a bit there*! like running over cat's eyes on the road when you start to fall asleep, a temporary wake up call, and all problems are only temporary, no matter how big you think they are; just a shove in the right direction, they can't last forever.

I'm starting to understand how important it is to just separate yourself from your life sometimes, just to put your mind right again. For me, my separation or buffer is Nature, it's like a deep form of meditation for me and that's one blessing that we have had the last few years. Being able to go away for weekends and just enjoy being in nature which would have been imposable for us just a few short years ago because of our financial situation.

I was thinking that I haven't really achieved that much over the past six years, but when I think about it, I have achieved a fair bit, even before I started writing this Journal, before I knew any of this way of thinking or more truthfully, started to remember what my Spirit has always known. Even when people don't realize who they really are, they still achieve things in life. A perfect example is a mate of mine who's a Builder. Even though he is doing pretty well financially, like everyone, he suffered through the Financial crisis but I hardly ever heard him say a negative thing, I think the most negative thing he said was... *"you know mate, I think this is the quietest I've been in 30 odd years"*. But even through those days he would ring me about a plastering job or something else and I'd ask him how he is, and he'd say... *"I woke up this morning mate so that's a good thing"*! And nearly every time I ring him, I ask him how he is and he says... *"I'm bloody fantastic Knoxie, how are you Mate"?*

Now he is so busy he can't keep up with it, just the other day he showed me his missed calls for that day, there was 54 missed calls on his phone which for a small business is a lot, considering through the financial crisis our phones wouldn't ring for sometimes a week or so at a time. As far as I know, he knows nothing about this way of thinking and from what I can see he's still achieved a fair bit in his life just from his positive attitude, so imagine what people could achieve if they woke up to who they really are, imagine the possibilities.

When I started writing this, Marina and I were looking at losing our house, our financial situation was not good to say the least and we were just sick of struggling all the time, but by changing the way we think and by starting to realize who we really are, and doing what we could from where we were, it started to turn our lives around. We are both different people from when we started and in a lot better place. A lot of things have gotten so much better over the past 6 years because of this Spiritual journey that we're both on.

20

My Biggest Challenge

8th October 2015

My biggest challenge in life has been my work life, by far. I was talking to my Mother on the phone just last night and she basically said that most of the grief I've had in my life comes back to work, the jobs I've had, and she's right. Even when it comes to the failed relationships I've had, a lot of the problems came from me being frustrated, angry and depressed and just feeling trapped a lot of the time because of work, not enjoying what I do. I think the closest I've ever been to being content with my job is having a trade and being my own boss, but I'm sure Marina gets sick of me saying... *"I'm frigg'n sick of my job"*!

Sometimes over the years I've thought to myself, *why can't you be like other people you know and just be happy with your job, or at least be content, like they are, just be happy you've got a job, or just be happy you've got a trade and you own your business*. I cover it up pretty well around people most of the time because they would probably think the same things and think, *just be happy with what you're doing,* but I can't, no matter how much self-talk I do, like... *you could be doing a lot worse things in life, you have a trade, you have your own business, you're your own boss...what's wrong with you!* That does work for a little while, but eventually I end up having the same negative feelings.

But from the things I've learnt over the past few years, I think everyone does have a Dharma, a life purpose, something their meant to achieve in their life, and I believe whatever it is, it will not only benefit yourself but also the people around you and I also believe that just by living your Devine purpose, a by- product of that is also living your dream life, because the Universe will open doors and bring things to you because you've found your Dharma. Can you imagine if everyone found their purpose in life which would not only benefit themselves but also the people around them, the Planet would be a much happy place, not to mention your own personnel world.

Maybe I just haven't found my life purpose yet.

I have always had this feeling that I'm meant to do something in life, a certain path I'm meant to follow and that's why I always, eventually, end up getting frustrated, angry and depressed with the jobs I've had because I'm not on the path I'm meant to be on. Then I see some people who are a lot younger then me who seem to have found their passion in life and I think, *maybe it's past me by, I'm 47 now so maybe I just didn't see the signs.* I've tried really hard to be open to signs from the Universe, especially since I've started this journey, and have tried

67

to stay conscious of things that interest and excite me but it hasn't happened yet, work wise anyway.

But then, I do believe in divine timing, it could be that it just hasn't been the right time yet, maybe everything I've experienced so far will one day all come together and I will find my Dharma. The hardest part is being patient, I've never been a patient person, that might be one thing the Universe is trying to get me to work on, if so…enough already!!

21

Devine Purpose

11th October 2015

You know, I have never written anything in my life, I have never even kept a diary even though my Mother use to try an encourage me to when I was younger, so reading back through some of my journal I was thinking...*who wrote this*? It doesn't seem like I wrote it when I read it, and then the thought crossed my mind that maybe my Dharma is staring me in the face, maybe part of my life purpose is to share my journey of slowly waking up to who I really am, of realizing that I am a piece of God, a powerful creator who can make my life the way I want it, after all, there would be so many people out there with a similar story to mine and similar challenges in their life and I have proven to myself that all of this is true, and if it's true for me (and Marina), it's true for everyone, because we all come from the same place, we are all a piece of God...made by, and of God, a part of the Universal energy that runs through everyone and everything in the Universe.

It's an old cliché but I can take the ribbing I'll get from my Mates (who knows, some of them might even start their own Journey of waking up to their selves), if people can get something helpful out of my Journey, that would really be something special.

I've also realized that I actually really enjoy writing and have enjoyed keeping this journal, I think it will be an ongoing thing for me now.

To top it all off, when we were at the Wayne Dyer Seminar in Brisbane, they had a table there with Information about a branch of the Hay House Company called *Balboa Press* which is a self-publishing Company. Marina filled out a form with our email address and our Information on it just to find out what it was about, she only put my name on the form, (bear in mind that Marina didn't know I was keeping this journal). Not long after thinking that maybe part of my life purpose might be to share my Story, I got an email from Alexa from Balboa Press with Information about the Company but also she asked...*Paul, I would be interested to know what your plans are for your book*!!

It amazes me sometimes how the Universe operates. The further we've got into our Spiritual journey, the more frequent these "coincidences" seem to happen.

My youngest Son, Dylan, rang me a few nights ago to have a chat. He finished high school a few year ago and he's been a bit lost, career wise. He's had a few different jobs. He started a painting apprenticeship, his older brother, Blaine, got him a job where he worked and he went to University for a while, but nothing has really sparked any interest or passion.

He has always been a gifted and talented sportsman, whatever sport he's played, he's excelled at but especially golf. My Mother's partner, Russell, put a golf club in his hands when he was about 4 years old, and he could actually hit the ball! Dylan has always had fantastic hand-eye coordination.

He started playing seriously when he was about 8, his Mother got him a membership at their local Golf Club, (he lived with her and I saw him every second weekend and half of all the school holidays) so he had a lot of support from her and I gave him as much support as I could. He started winning tournaments and got a Scholarship to a high school in Brisbane for Golf and was doing really well with it, He always use to tell me that he was going to be a pro Golfer when he grew up and I didn't doubt it because he definitely had the talent. But a few things happened in his life that put him off Golf for a while.

So, the other night when he rang he said- *"you know Dad, I've tried a few different things over the past couple of years and I've tried my best to stick it out, but it just turns into a nightmare, I just can't keep doing it. The only thing I love and am passionate about is Golf, I'm going to pursue my dream."*

I said to him that everyone is born with certain gifts and talents, things that just come natural that I believe your meant to use for your Life purpose, your given those gifts and talents for a reason and yours is sport.

Ever since my Sons were little, I always told them that I didn't care what they did in life as a career, as long as they love doing it, as long as Their passionate about it, because if you do that, all the material things will follow.

So I said to Dylan- *"that's great, it's fantastic, follow your dreams, if you follow your passions, you don't know what doors will open for you, I will support you has much as I can."*

My eldest Son, Blaine, loves his job, he done a green keeping apprenticeship at a Golf course after a few dead end jobs after he left School and is now a qualified green keeper. He has just finished working at a Golf course in New York (rent free) for 6 months, he was also given the opportunity to work in England for a while but decided to come back home. He's already got a job at a great Golf club when he gets home.

Now, Blaine didn't finish High School and he is travelling the World with his job. People might say- *well, he's just lucky,* and I say…*no, he loves his job and because of that doors have opened for him, but more than that, he had the courage to walk through those doors when the opportunity's come along.* And they will come along for Dylan as well, and every person who is following their passions, who are following their heart.

If your dream is to go to Uni, and your passionate about it, not because that's what other people want you to do, but because that's what you want to do, that's fantastic, go for it, there's a lot of support out there for people who want to go to Uni.

But I also want to give just as much support to the people who are following their passions that might not involve Uni. If you don't go to Uni, or even if you didn't finish High School, it's not the end of the world, there are so many very successful people in the World that didn't go to Uni and didn't finish High School.

When your lost and just don't know what to do anymore, follow your heart, follow your interests and passions, even if it's not a *"real job"* and doors will open up for you, you will find your path to your Devine purpose in life, your Dharma, just don't give up, keep your dreams alive, it will happen.

If you're in your 30's, 40's, 50's, 60's, 70's, or whatever decade you're in, re-kindle those dreams, those interests and passions, you don't have those dreams, interests and passions for no reason, and they don't stay with you during your life for no reason either, give them the attention and time they deserve, there your gifts from the Universe to follow.

Louise Hay started her very successful Company-*Hay House* when she was in her 60's, what an inspiration.

You don't know what doors the Universe will fling open for you to walk through by following you heart, and the Universe doesn't care about your age, whether you finished High School, whether you went to University or where you came from, once again, there physical insecurities, insecurities of the ego. Source energy just wants for you want you want for yourself, to be happy and abundant in all areas of life, that's our birthright, to live heaven on earth, as above, so below, all you have to do is have the courage to grab those opportunities the Universe sends you and walk through those doors when they open.

22

The Real Me

In hindsight, it makes sense now that a big part of my Dharma is writing. When I think about when I was younger and also throughout my life, I have always been an arty type person. When I was young I use to spend hours upon hours drawing and painting cartoons, it was my favorite past time. I have also been a thinker; I spend a lot of time thinking about numerous different things.

That's my personal side, the real me, the side most people didn't see. Most of the people around me seen the sporty me, the me that loved going out with his mates, getting drunk and having a good time, the me I showed people because that's who I thought they would like. Although I did enjoy those things when I was younger, it wasn't who I really was. The real person I am is an arty thinker who enjoys spending time in nature and thinking about the Spiritual side of things and the mysteries of life.

Writing is an art form and I believe people who spend a lot of time thinking should write their thoughts down, you don't have a lot of thoughts and spend time thinking about numerous different things for no reason, and the 30 odd years' experience of not liking what I did in my work life has given me plenty of things to write about and share with others. It has also given me the understanding and empathy for people who haven't found their Dharma yet, people who don't want to get out of bed in the morning because they hate the thought of going to work! And it has given me the motivation to help them because I know what it's like to not enjoy your work life, it can be a living nightmare!

So, what type of person are you? the real you, not the public you, not the you that all your friends see, the real you. Are you arty? Are you a thinker? Do you think a lot about numerous different things? Do you like using your hands, building things? Are you sporty? Do the mysteries of the world interest you? Are you a combination of some or maybe all of these thing?

That personal you is who you really are, the person you may not let many other people see. I tell you now, that person will give you clues as to what your Devine purpose is in this life. Be proud of it, of who you really are, follow it, if you lose friends because of being who you really are, then their purpose in your life has been fulfilled, let them go and move on to your purpose in life. Be who you really are, you won't find your Dharma, (and as a consequence of finding your divine purpose), live your dream life, any other way.

Over the years, accepting, acknowledging and honoring who I really am has been life transforming, it has let me discover my Dharma and in a few short weeks my interest in sharing my journey in the hope it will help and inspire others find their Dharma has turned into a passion- an obsession (in a good way).

I've found my Devine purpose, now I want to help others find theirs.

23

The Gift Of Experience

21st October 2015

It turns out that all the feelings of frustration, depression and feelings of feeling trapped over the last 30 odd years due to my work life was actually the gift of experience! All those times I woke up wishing I didn't, those thoughts that I was having a crappy life because of bad Karma, thinking I have to pay the Universe back for some miss deed in a past life, of thinking...*why are you doing this to me God!!* was all a Devine gift of experience. Because of that experience, I can now share it with other people who are going through the same thing in their work life, more importantly I understand how they are feeling and by sharing my journey I can help and hopefully inspire them to find their Devine purpose in life, their Dharma.

The Universe new what it was doing all along; giving me the experience I needed to share with other people so I could help them find their own Devine purpose. The big message in this is never...never ever give up! I'm 47 years old and I've only just found my Dharma. Now, instead of waking up wishing I didn't, I wake up so excited about writing and sharing my journey with other people and as a consequence, helping people find their Devine purpose.

Source energy truly does use people for a Devine purpose, it uses people as a tool to help others in their journey through this planet and as a byproduct of living your Dharma, you start living your dream life because you are on the path Source wants you to be on, the path you were born for, the Devine purpose you were sent here for to help others.

Now, to find my Dharma in life isn't just my reason for being here in this physical body, or for this person or that person, it's not just for the privileged people to find or the people who have had a lot of struggle in their lives, or for people who have a particular religious belief, a certain astrological chart, or whatever excuses you can think of as to why you're not living your dream life yet… yes…YET! It is for every single person on this planet to find their Devine purpose in life, no matter who you are or where you come from, so you can help others and as a consequence, live your dream life because when your living your Dharma, the Universe supports you, everything goes right in your life, things you need, the Universe will bring to you, exciting new doors will open for you to go through, all because you are doing what Source energy wanted for you before you came into this physical time and space World, and also what you wanted for yourself.

All these things are just starting to happen to me, and whatever anyone's Dharma is, you can be sure the result of following it will help other people, especially the people around you. If everyone on this planet were living their life purpose, can you imagine what the world would be like, it would be heaven on earth, they would all feel the excitement you will feel every day when you find your Dharma.

So, whatever you do, no matter how old or young you are or the circumstances your now in or what other people say...don't ever...ever give up, the Universe needs you, and so do other people. You are Source energy in physical form, you are Source's eye's, hands and ears. Like I said, every single person was sent here to find their Dharma, not just the lucky few...don't give up, if you give up, you can't help the people you were sent here to help.

When I say help, it's not just a physical thing, it could be that the paintings you paint make people feel good, it could be the poems you create make people feel loving, it could be a book you write will inspire people, it might be that the money you make when you find your Dharma will help people who need financial help, or, it might be physical, you might be a builder and build someone's dream home...you might build a lot of dream homes for people, you might be a Traddie who works on these dream houses to help bring them into the owner's reality. The only important thing is, you have to love what you do, you have to be passionate about it, if you're not, more than likely, it's not what you were born to do, it's not your Dharma.

Keep trying different things that excite you, try new experiences when they show up in your life, walk through doors that the Universe opens for you, but don't turn them into a cursed how. You don't know which of these interest the Universe will use to put you on your path to your Devine purpose. Eventually you will find your Dharma. It could be that your biggest challenge in your life might have something to do with your Devine purpose, embrace your circumstances and your challenges in life, they could be valuable tools to use when you find your Dharma, which will always be in Devine time.

My biggest challenge in life - my work life, turned out to be my most important and valuable gift from the Universe, those experiences and challenges had everything to do with my life purpose, my Dharma, and even though it seemed to take forever, and I got so impatient and frustrated a lot of the time, and just didn't want to get out of bed to face the day, it all happened when it was meant to, in Devine time, things wouldn't be the way they are if it was any earlier or any later…all in Devine time.

I've been on this Spiritual journey for 7 years now, so it's taken awhile to find my Devine purpose in life, my Dharma, and when I was in the thick of it, it felt like an eternity, but I remember reading something in one of Mike Dooley's books which said something like this- just keep going, keep trying from where you are, with what you have and always and only keep focused on the end result of what you want to achieve, not the how's, not the whys, not the when's, not the doubts that you can't do it, just what it will feel and look like when you've achieved your goal like it's already achieved, and don't give up, keep going, it will all happen in Devine time. After a while, you will reach critical mass, a point of no return, the flood gates will start to open, and your life will, (at first), start to trickle and then the gates will fly open and your life will take off!

When you really think about life, how amazing is it. Source energy gave us physical life from itself, we are God in physical form which gives us all the power we need to create. It gave us free will to choose whatever our heart desires to experience, it gave us dominion over all things so we can bring the experiences we want into our lives, whatever they are (*dominion over <u>All Things</u>!*) and to top it all off, we are eternal so there's no reason to fear anything, who we really are never dies. Man O man, how amazing is life!

But the reason there's so much suffering in the world, is because most people haven't woken up to themselves, they don't understand or believe in who they really are; a piece of God, Source energy in physical form with all the power they need to create whatever they want. Without belief, all the power in the Universe means nothing, it all means nothing without belief…You got to believe!

Marina and I have both grown so much, spiritually over the past seven years and because of that we can never go back to who we were, our lives have changed so much for the better because of our Spiritual growth, but this isn't the end, it is only just the start, things can only get better from here! The more we grow Spiritually, the more we wake up to ourselves… to who we really are, the better our lives will get... and so will yours if you start to discover and start believing in who you really are, I know that now for sure!

I better write an Introduction for my journal and send it to Alexa and see where it takes us

On with the Journey!

Notes

Notes

Notes

Notes

Notes

Printed in the United States
By Bookmasters